CAN I CROSS THE
SAHARA DESERT
IN ONE DAY?

EXPLORE THE DESERT GRADE 4 CHILDREN'S GEOGRAPHY & CULTURES BOOKS

First Edition, 2019

Published in the United States by Speedy Publishing LLC, 40 E Main Street, Newark, Delaware 19711 USA.

Baby Professor Books are available at special discounts when purchased in bulk for industrial and sales-promotional use. For details contact our Special Sales Team at Speedy Publishing LLC, 40 E Main Street, Newark, Delaware 19711 USA. Telephone (888) 248-4521 Fax: (210) 519-4043. www.speedybookstore.com

10 9 8 7 6 * 5 4 3 2 1

Print Edition: 9781541953529
Digital Edition: 9781541956520

See the world in pictures. Build your knowledge in style.
https://www.speedypublishing.com/

Table of Contents

The Sahara Desert

The Sahara Desert is one of the biggest, driest, hottest places on Earth! In this book, you will learn about the landscape, weather, animals, and people of the Sahara. Let's go explore the desert!

A Giant Desert

The Sahara is in northern Africa. It is the world's largest desert. In fact, the word "Sahara" means "desert" in Arabic. It covers an area of about 3.3 million square miles (8.6 million square kilometers). That's almost the size of the United States!

Sahara desert location

Sahara Desert Map

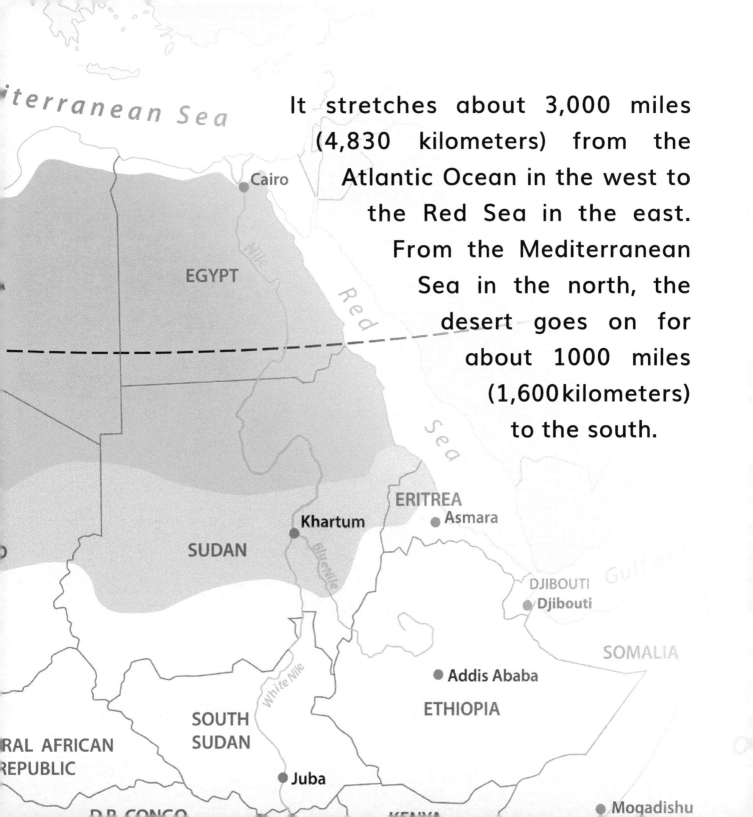

It stretches about 3,000 miles (4,830 kilometers) from the Atlantic Ocean in the west to the Red Sea in the east. From the Mediterranean Sea in the north, the desert goes on for about 1000 miles (1,600 kilometers) to the south.

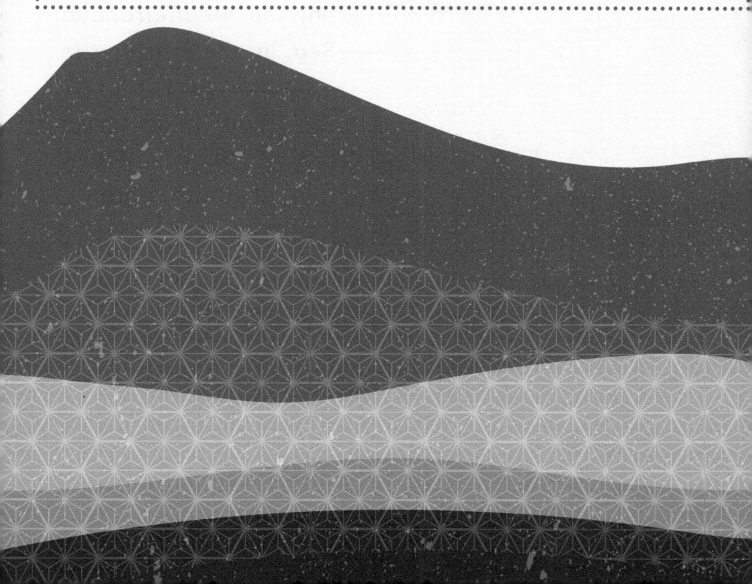

Mountains in the Desert

When you think of a desert, you probably think about sand, but deserts can have a lot of different landscapes. The Sahara is very rocky. There are mountains and high flat areas called plateaus.

Bizarre sandstone cliffs in Sahara Desert, Tassili N'Ajjer, Algeria

In the northwest, you can find the Atlas Mountains.

Desert road near Atlas Mountains, Morocco

The Ahaggar Mountains are located near the middle of the Sahara.

Ahaggar Mountain

The highest mountains in the Sahara are a little further east. They are called the Tibesti Mountains.

Tibesti Mountains

The highest place in the entire desert is a volcano called Emi Koussi. Its peak is 11,204 feet (3,415 meters) high! It isn't an active volcano, so it doesn't erupt anymore.

Emi Koussi Volcano

Finding Water

There are springs in the desert called oases. An oasis is an area where water comes up out of the rock deep underground. Sometimes villages and cities are built around oases because water is hard to find in the desert.

Oasis

More plants grow around oases and people can farm near them. About 750 miles (1,207 kilometers) of oases stretch from the Atlas Mountains to the Ahaggar Mountains.

More plants grow around oases and people can farm near them

Two rivers flow through the Sahara. A bend in the Niger River waters the desert in the southwest.

A panoramic view of the Niger River at sunset. Niamey, Niger, Africa

The world's longest river is the Nile. It flows up through the east side of the Sahara and empties out into the Mediterranean Sea. The areas around these rivers also make very good farmland.

Nile River

Another place where water can be found is called a wadi. Wadis are dry stream beds. Storms are rare in the desert but when they come, they fill the wadis with water.

Sahara wadi river

The water eventually seeps underground. Sometimes there are underground rivers beneath wadis. In fact, there are even deep underground lakes in the Sahara!

Sometimes there are underground rivers beneath wadis

Sand Dunes

Sand covers about one fourth of the Sahara desert. About half of that is made up of sand dunes. Sand dunes are formed when the wind blows sand into long, tall hills.

Sand dunes in the Sahara Desert, Merzouga, Morocco

The largest area of sand dunes is about the size of France! Sand may not seem like fertilizer but it actually has a lot of nutrients.

Weather

Sahara desert under the night starry sky

The temperature in the Sahara can drop to around 40°F (4°C) or less at night and reach over 120°F (49°C) during the day. The sand can get up to a scorching 170°F (77°C) or more!

This heat causes wind to blow. The hot air can create whirlwinds called waltzing jinns. Another word for "jinn" is "genie".

Waltzing jinn or "genie"

Sometimes very strong winds blow and pick up sand. These winds become sandstorms. Sandstorms can grow to a height of 3,300 feet (1,000 meters) and are very dangerous.

Sandstorm on sand dunes of the Sahara Desert, Morocco

Sandstorms aren't all bad though. They pick up a lot of small dust particles and send them high into the atmosphere.

Sandstorm

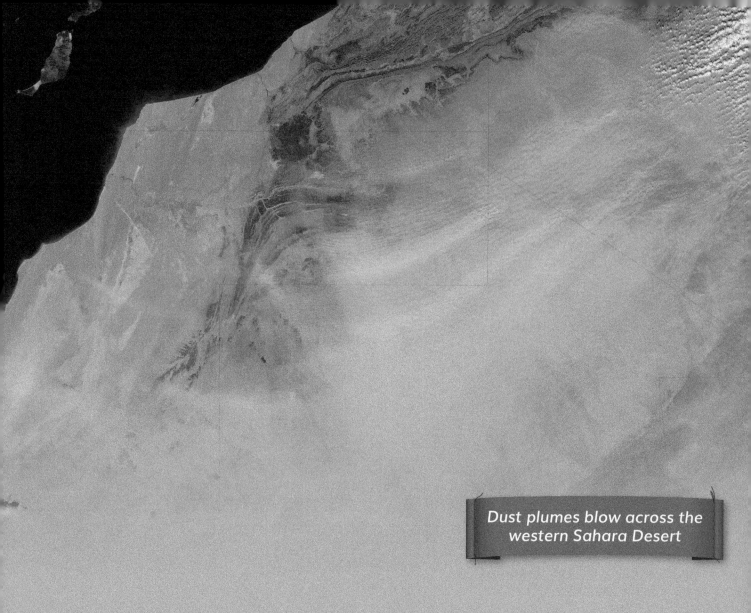

Dust plumes blow across the western Sahara Desert

These dust clouds can weigh a million tons and cover an area of 193,000 square miles (500,000 square kilometers)! The dust clouds help to form rain clouds as they float over the Atlantic Ocean.

When the clouds reach South America, the nutrients from the Sahara rain down on the Amazon rainforest!

NASA satellite image reveals how much Saharan dust feeds the plants in the Amazon rainforest

Rain is rare in the Sahara but when it rains, it pours! Sometimes 10 years or more will pass before a rainstorm comes.

Thunderclouds in the desert during a storm

When it rains, the wadis flood and flowers quickly grow and bloom in the desert.

Pool of water after the storm

Plants and Animals

The Sahara wasn't always a desert. In fact, it used to be a grassland. Even fossilized trees have been found in the desert!

Tree Log From The North Sahara Desert

Broken pieces of fossilised tree trunks

Today, tough grasses grow in thick clumps here and there. You can also find drought and heat resistant shrubs in the desert. Acacia, olive, cypress, and palm trees also grow in some places.

Tough grasses grow in Sahara desert in Tunisia, Africa

Plants in the Sahara often have deep roots that can reach underground water. Some plants only grow near oases, where water is plentiful.

Some plants only grow near oases

The desert may seem like a hard place to live but many animals make their home in the Sahara.

A herd of animals living in the Sahara Desert in Niger, Agadez, Africa

Gazelles, gerbils, baboons, foxes, hedgehogs, hyenas, and wild donkeys are just some of the mammals that live in the Sahara.

Gazelles

Gerbils

Baboon

Fox

Hedgehog

Hyenas

Wild Donkey

Over 300 species of birds also live in the desert. Eagles, owls, ravens, and ostriches are just a few.

Eagle

Owl

Raven

Ostrich

Frogs, toads, and crocodiles live around some oases and lakes. Snakes, lizards, scorpions, ants, and even snails survive in the Sahara.

Frog   Crocodile   Snake

Lizard   Scorpion   Snail

Desert People

The Sahara desert stretches across parts of 10 different countries. Cities are usually built around the edges of the desert or near oases.

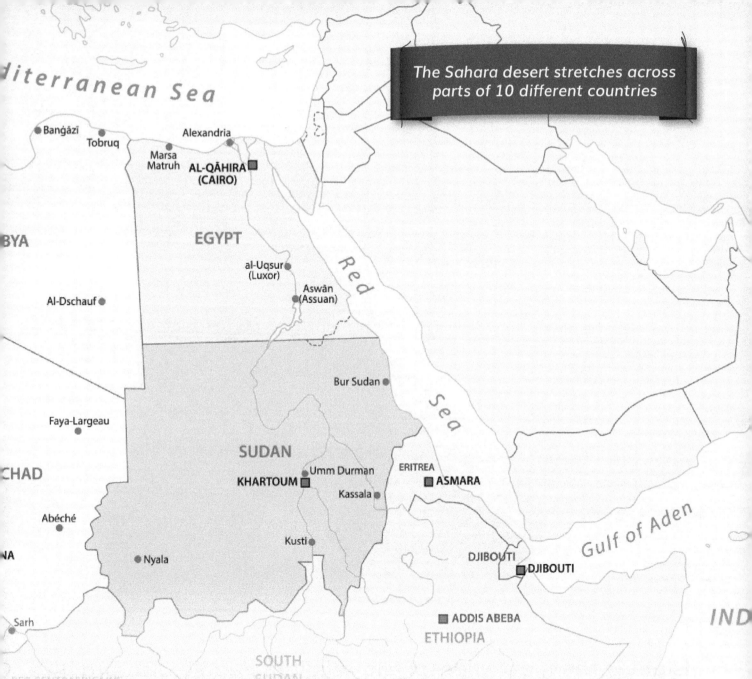

Arabic is the main language in most of the Sahara. French, English, and various tribal languages are also spoken.

Islam is the most widespread
religion in Sahara

Islam is the most widespread religion. People also practice
Christianity or tribal religions in some places.

Farming, Mining, and Manufacturing

Farming is a big business for cities in the Sahara. They grow fruits like oranges, mangoes, grapes, watermelons, dates, and olives.

Fresh produce at an Arabian marketplace near the Sahara Desert

Many vegetables are grown as well. Some of these are: cassava, sweet potatoes, onions, tomatoes, potatoes, and sugar beets.

Rice, millet, sorghum, barley, corn, and wheat are some of the grains grown there. Beans, cotton, sugarcane, and peanuts are also major crops.

Sahara Farmers

The Sahara has a lot of minerals. People mine for gold, coal, zinc, manganese, limestone, salt, and iron ore. They also drill for oil and natural gas.

Mining in the Sahara

Manufactured goods also come from the desert. Clothing, shoes, cloth, bricks, and tiles are a few. Tourism is important in some countries.

Sahara Natural Resources

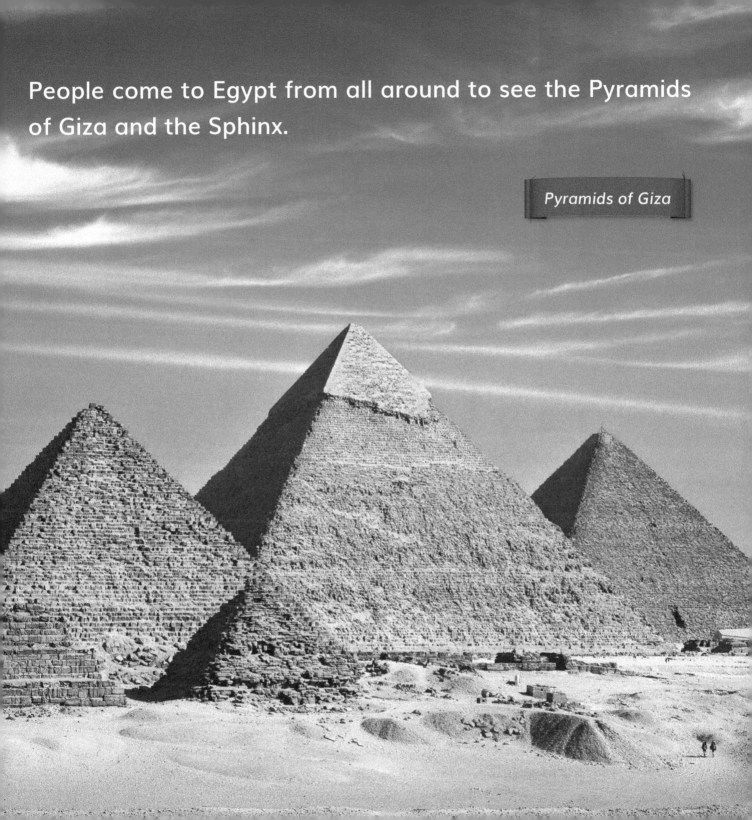

People come to Egypt from all around to see the Pyramids of Giza and the Sphinx.

Pyramids of Giza

Nomads

Nomads are people who travel from place to place and live in tents instead of houses. The Sahara has many nomads. One group is called the Berbers.

Group of red nomad tents around courtyard, Berber camp in Sahara desert, Morocco

They herd sheep, goats, and camels. Berbers wear long thick robes to protect themselves from the sun and the sand. They also wear turbans on their heads and sandals on their feet.

Berbers with Dromadaires in Sahara Desert Morocco

When they come to a village or city, they bring cheese made from goat or camel milk and animal skins to trade.

Berbers come to a village to trade

Nomads have lived in the desert for thousands of years. They know how to survive there.

Berbers lived in the desert for thousand of years

They don't get lost even though the desert changes all the time. They know the best places to find water and the safest routes to travel. This makes them the best guides in the Sahara!

They know the best places to find water and the safest routes to travel.

Summary

The Sahara desert is in northern Africa, and it is the biggest desert in the world. It is very rocky in places and has mountains and plateaus. Sand covers about one fourth of the desert.

Sahara Desert at night

Water is scarce in the Sahara. There are only two rivers that run through it. Most of the water comes from underground springs called oases. Water can also be found in wadis, places where floodwater gathers after a rainstorm. In some parts of the desert, it may rain only once every 10 years or more.

It can be very hot in the desert during the day and very cold at night. Sometimes strong winds pick up sand and become sandstorms. The dust that flies high into the atmosphere helps to make clouds which fertilize the Amazon rainforest in South America.

Tough trees and plants with deep roots grow in the Sahara. All kinds of mammals, birds, reptiles, amphibians, and insects survive in the desert.

The Sahara covers at least part of 10 different countries. Most of the people speak Arabic but some people speak French, English, or tribal languages. Islam is the main religion but Christianity and tribal religions also exist.

People who live in cities and villages near water may be farmers, miners, factory workers, or tour guides. Farmers grow fruits, vegetables, grains, and other crops. Miners dig up minerals and drill for oil and natural gas. Other workers make cloths and tiles or give tours of famous monuments.

Nomads are people who live in tents in the desert. They travel from place to place with herds of sheep, goats, and camels in search of fresh grass and water. They make cheese and animal skins to trade for things they need from cities and villages.

Sahara Desert

Now that you've traveled across the Sahara in one day, you probably want to learn about other deserts! Try The Six Largest Deserts in the World! Geography Books for Kids 5-7 | Children's Geography Books or Most Dangerous Deserts In The World | Deserts Of The World for Kids | Children's Explore the World Books by Baby Professor.

Visit

www.BabyProfessorBooks.com

to download Free Baby Professor eBooks and view our catalog of new and exciting Children's Books

Ingram Content Group UK Ltd.
Milton Keynes UK
UKHW051911060323
418097UK00003B/22